# SUMM

CW01024226

## TO

# Colorless TsukuruTazaki and His Years of Pilgrimage

## Haruki Murakami

**TRIVIA EDITION COLLECTION**

## By WhizBooks

**Please Note: This is an unofficial trivia on books. If you have not yet read the original work or would like to read it again, <u>get the book here.</u>**

# Before We Begin

Dear reader,

To say thank you,

We've included a free gift download of our *All-Time Top 5 Bestselling* Guides for you absolutely free.

To access your free bonus gifts enter your email for an instant delivery of our *All-Time Top 5 Bestselling* titles to your inbox.

<u>Enter Best Email Address Here</u>

We hope you will enjoy this book. Don't forget to keep score, and then challenge your friends and family.

What will your trivia score be?

Editor at
# WhizBooks

# Table of Contents

# Round One: Set Go

## *"Ready to start the challenge?"*

## 1 POINT EACH

# Question #1

**The main character of *Colorless Tsukuru Tazaki and His Years of Pilgrimage* is a man named Tsukuru Tazaki. What is the meaning of his name?**

a. "to put together"

b. "to blend in"

c. "to make or build"

d. "to stand out"

# ANSWER c

## "to make or build"

TsukuruTazaki means "to make or build" in Japanese, which is fitting for his character since his love for train stations eventually led him to become an engineer and work for a company that builds train stations. In the present time, he is 36-years-old and still emotionally scarred from being ostracized by his close high school friends during his second year in college. They cut all ties with him via phone calls and stopped visiting him. The disappearance of another close friend in college made him further depressed, confused, and suicidal. He sets out on a journey to make peace with himself and his friends and find out the reason why they suddenly gave him the cold shoulder.

# Question #2

## Why does Tsukuru consider himself plain and colorless compared to his friends?

a.   He can't see a person's color aura like them.

b.   His name doesn't contain any color, and he is

plain compared to them.

c.   All of them are on the same sports team

except him.

d.   They all play a musical instrument, and he

doesn't.

# ANSWER b

His name doesn't contain any color, and he is plain compared to them.

Tsukuru now lives in Tokyo and is dating Sara Kimoto. During one of their discussions during dinner, he related to her about his high school friends. All of them had nicknames that were after the colors found in their surnames. He was the colorless one in the group, the plain one against the colorful personality of his friends. He told her how close they were and how they did everything together that the absence of one would instantly be noticed. He received a phone call one day from his friends that they did not want to see him or do anything with him again. No explanation, no cruel words were exchanged, just that declaration and nothing else. Tsukuru was stunned and distraught with the abrupt decision but did not ask why.

# Question #3

**Tsukuru befriended someone in college, but he disappeared just before the beginning of the second semester. Who was this person?**

a.  FumiyakiHaida

b.  Kei Akamatsu

c.  Yoshio Oumi

d.  Midorikawa

# ANSWER a

## FumiyakiHaida

F umiyakiHaida is one of the few people that Tsukuru was able to befriend in college. His name also contains color as his family name means "Gray Paddy" in Japanese. Though he is two years younger than Tsukuru, they were able to connect with each other and became close. They were inseparable and listened to classical music together. One day, he slept over at Tsukuru'splace and woke up the following morning to find that Haida was nowhere to be found. Only a boxed set of *Years of Pilgrimage* was left, which he had lent

Tsukuru. Tsukuru wondered about Haida'swhereabouts;

he felt estranged once again when Haida did not show up

the next semester.

# Question #4

**Who was the jazz pianist that Haida's father met while working at an isolated hot spring?**

a. Hiroshi

b. Shinagawa

c. Kazuma

d. Midorikawa

# ANSWER d

## Midorikawa

One evening, Haida shared with Tsukuru about Midorikawa, a very talented jazz pianist from Tokyo whose surname means "Green River". While taking a break from his college studies, Haida's father was able to work at a secluded hot spring, which was where his father met Midorikawa. He was so incredibly talented that his playing would take you to another world. He has one habit however, that people find puzzling--he always placed a small bag on the piano before he started to play. The bag's content was never revealed in the novel. Midorikawa shared a strange story about himself about how he came upon a "death token" that destined him to die in two months, unless he passed it on. Despite his talent, he was a heavily burdened man, and as he was nearing his death, he confessed that he was able to see the color aura of people.

# Question #5

## Who is Tsukuru's love interest in the book?

a. YuzukiShirane

b. Sara Kimoto

c. EriKurono

d. Yoshio Oumi

# ANSWER b

## Sara Kimoto

Sara Kimoto is Tsukuru's love interest; she is beautiful and Tsukuru has a strong desire for her. Sara works at a travel agency and is two years older than Tsukuru. On their fourth date, Sarah probes Tsukuru to reveal more information about his past and he opens up about his four high school friends in Nagoya and how they estranged him one day. She encouraged Tsukuru to be at terms with his past and move on and not be a "wounded little boy" but man up to face it. Later on, Tsukuru finds Sara with another man as he was preparing for his trip to Finland, which saddened him.

Upon his return, he asked if she was seeing someone else

and her reply was for him to wait three days for an answer.

**Who called to tell Tsukuru about the group's decision not to see him anymore?**

a. Ao

b. Aka

c. Shiro

d. Kuro

# ANSWER a

## Ao

Yoshio Oumi or Ao informed Tsukuru about the group's decision to cut ties with him. When Tsukuru came home from the university, he noticed that his friends started to ignore him. He tried to ask them why they were avoiding him but a call came from Ao telling him that they didn't want to be associated with him anymore. He told Tsukuru not to call or come see any of them. Tsukuru asked what he did to offend them, but Ao tells him vaguely that he should already know the reason, which left Tsukuru even more confused. This became a huge blow to Tsukuru's already deflated ego and 16 years later, he is still haunted by it.

**Kei Akamatsu or Aka, as Tsukuru fondly calls him, tells him about a personal secret when he came over to visit. What was his secret?**

    a.  That he raped Shiro

    b.  That he killed Shiro

    c.  That he is gay

    d.  That he was the one who convinced the others to

        banish Tsukuru

# ANSWER c

That he is gay

Kei Akamatsu or Aka (Red), whose surname means "Red Pine", is now a successful business owner. Many thought that he would become a college professor due to his intelligence and logical thinking. Instead, he dropped out of college and decided to pursue a career in the corporate world. He runs a company that offers management training seminars for big companies. Though he is largely successful, he is unhappy. He revealed to Tsukuru about Shiro losing the will to live even before she died. He also tells him that he is gay, something he realized after a failed marriage. He felt confined and rejected in Nagoya, especially with Ao's treatment towards him.

**Where did Tsukuru meet the last member of their group, EriKurono, now a successful pottery artist?**

a. Ten years

b. Eleven years

c. Twelve years

d. Thirteen years

# ANSWER a

## Hameenlinna, Finland

EriKurono (Kuro), which means "Black Meadow", was the sarcastic yet sharp-witted member of the group. She now lives in Finland with her family. She fell in love with a foreign student named EdvardHaatainen, who came to Japan to study pottery. Tsukuru met Kuro's husband first at their holiday college in Hameenlinna. She arrived later on along with her two daughters. Edvard took the girls and left the two behind so they could talk. She explains to Tsukuru about Shiro's deteriorating mental health and that the rape accusation was all made up by her. She also tells Tsukuru that she was in love with him before, but she decided it was best that she did not confess to him about her feelings.

**What did Shiro tell the others that led them to shun Tsukuru from their group?**

a. She accused Tsukuru of backstabbing them.

b. She accused Tsukuru of raping her.

c. She accused Tsukuru of stealing something from

her.

d. She accused Tsukuru of befriending criminals.

# ANSWER b

She accused Tsukuru of raping her.

Yuzuki Shirane is nicknamed Shiro, which means "White" in Japanese. Her family name means "White Root" in Japanese. She is described as extremely beautiful with long black hair. She hated the attention she got from her looks and enjoyed playing the piano. She did not become a concert pianist but did become a private piano teacher. She has the most tragic fate among the group; she was strangled to death, and her murder remains unsolved six years later. She accused Tsukuru of raping her while she went to

Tokyo, but none of them believed her. Though the accusation was false, it was Kuro who revealed to Tsukuru that she was indeed raped and had a miscarriage. She then became anorexic and mentally unstable. The group did not want to involve Tsukuru as well to protect Shiro's fragile state of mind. The group thought of Tsukuru as the strongest one emotionally and that he could deal with the rejection.

# Question #10

## What was the title of the musical piece that was repeatedly mentioned in the novel?

a. Fur Elise

b. Clair de Lune

c. Le mal du pays

d. Plaisird'amour

# ANSWER c

## Le mal du pays

"**A**nnées de pèlerinage" (Years of Pilgrimage) is a compilation of piano pieces by Franz Liszt, including the haunting piece called*Lche mal du pays*, which means "homesickness". It's a melancholic song that reflects the person's emptiness. The song is a recurring motif in the novel; it was first mentioned when Shiro plays the tune on the piano. Tsukuru and Haida often listened to classical music together. Before Haida disappeared, he leaves a copy of "Years of Pilgrimage" behind. Tsukuru seems to be captivated by it; it was written in the novel that he listened to it over and over again. Kuro also owns a recording.

# Round Two: Getting Harder

*"Let's get personal."*

## 2 POINTS EACH

# Question #1

**Who was the author of *Colorless TsukuruTazaki and His Years of Pilgrimage*?**

a. Kenzaburo Oe

b. Banana Yoshimoto

c. NatsuoKirino

d. Haruka Murakami

# ANSWER d

## Haruka Murakami

Haruka Murakami is a Japanese writer who was born in Kyoto. He is a novelist as well as a short story writer. His works are bestsellers and have been translated into 50 languages and distributed worldwide. He has garnered global recognition as a bestselling author with his books selling millions of copies internationally. His fiction and non-fiction works have been given critical acclaim both in his native country and abroad. He was named as one of *TIMEMagazine*'s 100 most influential people in April 2015.

# Question #2

**While watching a baseball game, Murakami got the sudden urge and inspiration to write a novel. What was the first novel that Murakami wrote?**

a. *Kafka by the Shore*

b. *Pinball, 1973*

c. *Norwegian Wood*

d. *Hear the Wind Sing*

# ANSWER d

*Hear the Wind Sing*

While watching a baseball game between the Yakult Swallows and Hiroshima Carp at the Jingu Stadium in 1978, Murakami came to witness Dave Hilton, an American, hit a double. The instant that Hilton hit that double was when Murakami realized that he wanted to write a novel - and so he did. He went home and started to write that night. He worked on what would be his first novel, Hear the Wind Sing for ten months while working at his jazz bar.

He sent it to one literary contest who would accept the novel despite its length, and it won the first prize.

**Hear the Wind Sing, Pinball, 1973 and A Wild Sheep Chase form Murakami's first trilogy. What is the title of this trilogy?**

a. *Dance, Dance, Dance*

b. *The Trilogy of the Rat*

c. *The Elephant Vanishes*

d. *Blind Willow, Sleeping Woman*

# ANSWER b

*The Trilogy of the Rat*

After his success with *Hear the Wind Sing*, Murakami was encouraged and wrote his second novel, which happens to be a sequel of his first work. *Pinball, 1973* was published in 1980 and was followed by another sequel, *A Wild Sheep Chase*, which was a massive success. *Dance, Dance, Dance* followed later but is not considered part of the trilogy. All of the books are centered on a nameless narrator and his friend he calls "the Rat". Though the novels were a huge hit in Japan, Murakami refused to have the first two published in English. He thinks that his first two novels are "immature" and "flimsy". He first felt the "joy of telling a story" with his third novel, *A Wild Sheep Chase.*

**Aside from being a writer, Murakami is also a sports' fan. What was the first sporting event that he participated in?**

a. Swimming

b. Boxing

c. Biking

d. Triathlon running

# ANSWER d

## Triathlon running

Murakami is a running and triathlon enthusiast. He was able to complete his first ultra marathon, whichwas held at Lake Saroma in Hokkaido, Japan on June 23, 1996. The ultramarathon is one of the longest triathlon races; it covers a 100-kilometer distance. Though he is an avid fan of running, he did not start training and running until he was 33-years-old. In his memoir, *What I Talk About When I Talk About Running*, which was published on 2008, he shares his passion and relationship with running. In the book, he revealed that he started running in the early 1980s and has since participated in over 20 marathons and ultra marathons.

# Question #5

**Murakami published a book that was a collection of seventeen short stories all written by him. What is the title of this book?**

a. *Blind Willow, Sleeping Woman*

b. *The Elephant Vanishes*

c. *Men Without Women*

d. *After Dark*

# ANSWER b

## *The Elephant Vanishes*

*T*he Elephant Vanishes is a collection of 17 short stories written by Murakami. Some of these stories were already released to different publications and magazines in Japan. They were written between 1980 and 1991 and have Murakami's distinct style and themes in writing such as surrealism and melancholy. The stories were picked by Gary Fisketjon and were first published in English in 1993. Before that, the translations for some of these stories already appeared in publications such as *The New Yorker*, *Playboy,* and *The*

*Magazine.* The Japanese version was released in 2005. *The Elephant Vanishes* is the last short story in the collection.

# Question #6

**Murakami expresses his interest in this kind of music. Some of the titles of his books were even hailed from it. What type of music was repetitively mentioned in his novels?**

a. Classical music

b. Country music

c. Rock music

d. Jazz music

# ANSWER a

## Classical music

Many of Murakami's books have mentioned classical music as a theme or backdrop of the settings including: *The Wind-Up Bird Chronicle: The Thieving Magpie,* which came from Rossini's opera; *Bird as Prophet*, a piano piece by Robert Schumann also known as *The Prophet Bird*; and *"The Bird Catcher"* a character from Mozart's opera, *The Magic Flute.* These three books comprise Murakami's *The Wind-Up Bird Chronicle.* In his novel, *Colorless Tsukuru Tazaki and His Years of Pilgrimage,* the "Années de pèlerinage" or *Years of Pilgrimage* by Franz Liszt was mentioned several times including the piece *Le mal du pays,* which means "homesickness."

In 2011, Murakami released another novel that became a huge hit. It's a fiction novel with supernatural elements. What is the title of this novel?

a. *Kafka on the Shore*

b. *Sputnik Sweetheart*

c. *1Q84*

d. *South of the Border, West of the Sun*

## *1Q84*

*1Q84* is a supernatural and suspense novel by Murakami, which earned critical acclaim in Japan and internationally. It was published in three volumes, Book 1 and Book 2 on May 29, 2009, and Book 3 on April 16, 2010. It became a sensation with the first prints being sold out on the first day of its release and reaching one million dollars in sales in just a month. The English translation was published in one volume on October 25, 2011. The first two books were translated by Jay Rubin and the third one by Philip Gabriel. It took

Murakami four years to finish the novel. Murakami did not reveal much information about it and the details were vague, but there was still a large demand for reservations and advanced orders following his announcement.

# Question #8

## What biennial literary award did Murakami receive in January 2009?

a. Gunzo Award

b. Jerusalem Prize

c. World Fantasy Award

d. Franz Kafka Prize

# ANSWER b

## Jerusalem Prize

Murakami was given the Jerusalem Prize in January 2009. It's an award given twice a year to writers who include themes such as human freedom, politics, government, and society in their works. The Japanese were against his attending the award ceremony in February due to the recent incident of Israel bombing Gaza. Some even expressed their sentiment by threatening to boycott his works. However, Murakami still pushed through and attended the ceremony but gave a speech that criticized

Israeli policies in front of the Israeli dignitaries present at the ceremony. He stated that each of us (people) possesses a soul, but the system does not hold such things and that we must not allow this kind of system to exploit us.

**Which of Murakami's books turned him into a "superstar sensation" to the youth of Japan?**

a. *Norwegian Wood*

b. *Hard-Boiled Wonderland and the End of the World*

c. *Sputnik Sweetheart*

d. *1Q84*

# ANSWER a

*Norwegian Wood*

The Japanese title *Noruwei o Mori* is the direct translation of the Beatles song, *Norwegian Wood (This Bird Has Flown)*, another Murakami book that inspired its title from a song. It's also the favorite song of one of the characters in the book, Naoko. Mori means wood or "forest" and not the material. Therefore, the forest setting in the book is very significant to the novel. It was published in 1987 and was very popular with the Japanese youth. It propelled his career to superstar status in his native country. As with other

Murakami novels, the story is told from a first person perspective. The narrator is Toru Watanabe, who reminisces about the time he had during his college years and of the relationships he had then. The book is available in two different volumes, Red and Green, which helped double its sales.

**How much did Murakami donate for the relief and victims of the 2011 earthquake and tsunami that hit Tōhoku, Japan?**

a. €20,000

b. €40,000

c. €80,000

d. €100,000

€80,000

Murakami was able to win the International Catalunya Prize in 2011. He donated all the proceeds of his €80,000 winnings to the Tōhoku earthquake and tsunami victims, including those affected by the Fukushima nuclear disaster. During his speech, he expressed his disapproval of the occurrence at Fukushima and he stated that this was the second major nuclear disaster that happened in Japan, and it was done by the Japanese people. According to Murakami, they should have rejected the use of nuclear power having learned from the

past at how badly it can affect the people and how the scars

from radiation can run deep.

# Reminder: Claim Your Books

Dear reader,

If you haven't already, don't forget to claim your free download of our *All-Time Top 5 Bestselling* Guides for you absolutely free as a part of this purchase.

Just enter where you want the books to be digitally delivered.

Enter Best Email Address Here

We hope you will enjoy this book.

What will your trivia score be?

Editor at
## WhizBooks

# Round Three: Enter Fan Zone

*"Are you a true fan?"*

## 3 POINTS EACH

# Question #1

***Colorless TsukuruTazaki and His Years of Pilgrimage*** **is the _____ novel by Haruka Murakami.**

a. Fifth

b. Ninth

c. Thirteenth

d. Fifteenth

# ANSWER c

## Thirteenth

*C*olorless *TsukuruTazaki and His Years of Pilgrimage* is Murakami's 13<sup>th</sup>novel. It was released on April 12, 2013, in Japan and sold over million copies in just a month after its release. On August 12, 2014, the English version was released and was translated by Philip Gabriel. It eventually topped the US bestsellers lists of *BookScan*, *New York Times* and *NPR* under the "hardcover fiction" genre. On Feburary, the book was announced to be released in April while in March, only the title and release date were disclosed.

# Question #2

**What was the exact date that *Colorless TuskuruTazaki and His Years of Pilgrimage* set to be released in Japan?**

a.  April 12, 2013

b.  May 12, 2013

c.  August 12, 2013

d.  September 12, 2013

# ANSWER a

## April 12, 2013

The book's release date was to be midnight on April 12, 2013. Though it was rather unconventional, many people have lined up to purchase the book. Many late night bookstores in Tokyo have seen a long line of more than 150 people trying to get a copy of Murakami's book. The bookstores started selling the book at 12:00 a.m. and a week after its release, the book had sold over a million copies in Japan alone and had been printed eight times over in the same month. In November, a point-of-sale information firm, Oricon, certified a more detailed statistic of the sales, stating that

the book has sold over 985,000 copies.

**From which non-profit media organization did**
***Colorless TuskuruTazaki and His Years of Pilgrimage***
**stay in the Top 15 for 18 weeks?**

a. BookScan

b. The New York Times

c. iDreamBooks

d. NPR

# ANSWER d

## NPR

*C*olorless *Tsukuru and His Years of Pilgrimage* ranked in National Public Radio's Top 15 and stayed there for 18 weeks. It was listed #1 for the first three weeks. The book also topped other US bestseller lists in its first week. It stayed four weeks in *BookScan*'s Top 10 and in the *New York Times*' Top 20 as well and stayed eight weeks on their list. It also peaked on *iDreamBook*'s Top 25 "Fiction Bestsellers" and was #5 for two weeks. Murakami showed his support of the international launchings and even went to two public appearances in the UK for signing and an open talk on August 23-24, 2014 at the Edinburgh International Book Festival in Scotland and a signing event held at Piccadilly bookstore in London on August 30.

# Question #4

**How many pages is the Japanese hardcover of**
*Colorless TsukuruTazaki and His Years of Pilgrimage?*

a. 370 pages

b. 386 pages

c. 298 pages

d. 275 pages

# ANSWER a

## 370 pages

T he Japanese hardcover version of *Colorless TsukuruTazaki and His Years of Pilgrimage* has 370 pages, the United States version has 386 pages, and the United Kingdom release has 298 pages. The book was first released in hardcover in Japan and the English translation was released in all formats including print, digital, and audio. Many people lined up in bookstores and others signed up for pre-orders as well. The bookwas received well by both critics and readers alike, and it has added to Murakami's popularity as a writer.

**Colorless TsukuruTazaki and His Years of Pilgrimage is considered to be a bildungsroman kind of novel. What does bildungsroman mean in literature?**

    a. Supernatural story

    b. Romance story

    c. Coming of age story

    d. Country life story

# ANSWER c

## Coming of age story

*C*olorless *TsukuruTazaki and His Years of Pilgrimage* is a bildungsroman novel yet the more realist kind, as many denote that the supernatural happenings were either dreams or tales. A bildungsroman novel relates to the "coming of age" or "growing up" of a person; most of these people will go on a journey in search of life's questions that will help him gain experience to change his outlook of himself and the world. TsukuruTazaki, the narrator and main protagonist of the novel, sets out on a pilgrimage to find answers from a series of events that happened 16 years ago to finally be

at peace with himself and understand the past.

**How many chapters is*Colorless Tsukuru Tazaki and His Years of Pilgrimage?***

    a.  Thirteen chapters

    b.  Fifteen chapters

    c.  Nineteen chapters

    d.  Twenty-one chapters

# ANSWER c

## Nineteen chapters

*C*olorless *Tsukuru Tazaki and His Years of Pilgrimage* is composed of nineteen chapters. The story begins with Tsukuru Tazaki, a 36-year-old man with a wounded past. He talks about his life in Nagoya and his four best friends in high school. Their group is composed of two girls and two boys who are either smart, talented, or blessed with good looks. Compared to the four, he seems like someone who belongs in the background. The first three chapters follow Tsukuru as he looks back into his past, and all that has happened: from his four close friends in high school until he left for college and his best friends ceased all contact with him so suddenly that it left him shocked and confused.

**Which review stated that *Colorless TsukuruTazaki and His Years of Pilgrimage*is "hypnotically" engaging?**

a. Kirkus

b. Booklist

c. Elle Magazine

d. Library Journal

# ANSWER b

## Booklist

*ooklist* is an online magazine that publishes book reviews in different genres as well as offers recommendations, articles, and lists of awards in literature. According to *Booklist*'s review of the novel, it was "hypnotically" engaging. They congratulate Murakami for writing yet another warm and poignant story. In their full review, they described *Colorless Tsuzuki and His Years of Pilgrimage* as a metaphysical novel with a complex narrative has become a worldwide bestseller. It may baffle one's mind as to how a book could sell a million copies in a week. It is also inspiring as the novel itself is "devilishly difficult" yet "hypnotically fascinating."

**Which online website gave *Colorless Tsuzuki Tazaki and His Years of Pilgrimage* a rating of four out of five stars?**

a. Kirkus

b. The New York Times

c. Goodreads

d. Entertainment Weekly

# ANSWER c

## Goodreads

On the *Goodreads* website, the book was able to get four out of five stars from its readers. There are many reviews onthe site, and most of them are mixed--some positive, some negative, and some are confused as to how they rate the novel. Many of those who left reviews have read at least one of Murakami's works, and there are those that have been convinced by the hype to buy it. Many find that the novel has fallen short since they expected something more on surrealism and fantasy that Murakami typically includes in his novels. However, there are those that liked the novel the way it is; there's even a comparison to it over his previous novel *Norwegian Wood*--they are both coming of age stories and deal with the loss of innocence.

# Question #9

## Which chapter of the book became a standalone and published on Slate?

a. Chapter 1

b. Chapter 7

c. Chapter 9

d. Chapter 5

# ANSWER d

## Chapter 5

Chapter 5 or "Haida's Story" is an excerpt from *Colorless Tsuzuki and His Years of Pilgrimage* and was published on *Slate* on July 27, 2014, as a standalone story. Haida is a character from the novel in which the protagonist became close to. Tsuzuki Tazaki, the narrator, became friends with Haida, who is two years younger than him while he was in college. They became close friends quickly and just like Tazaki did with his friends in high school, they did things together such as listening to classical music. However, before the start of the second semester in college, Haida disappeared, leaving Tsuzuki very much alone and rejected once again.

**Which book reviewer and author said that *Colorless Tsuzuki Tazaki and His Years of Pilgrimage* is "fascinating, exquisite, and emotional"?**

    a.  Jake Kerridge

    b.  Boris Kachka

    c.  EithneFarry

    d.  Sean O'Hagan

# ANSWER c

## EithneFarry

E ithneFarry stated in her review of *Colorless Tsuzuki Tazaki and His Years of Pilgrimage* that the novel is "fascinating, exquisite, and emotional." EithneFarry is a British book reviewer and *ELLE* magazine's former literary editor. She also authored books such as *Yeah, I Made it Myself: DIY fashion for the not very domestic goddess* (2006) and *Lovely Things to Make for Girls of Slender Means* (2010). She also co-authored a book with Philipp Dodd, Michael Heatley, and Martin Noble entitled *Encyclopedia of Singles*. She has worked for *Marie Claire* and the *Daily Mail* as a literary critic. Aside from that, she has had a string of jobs ranging from being a backup singer to becoming a radio personality.

# The Moment of Truth

## *Results May Vary*

**Based on the difficulty of the questions you are an Avid Fan if you've scored more than "41" points.**

# Play Again?

## The First Challenge

## The Second Challenge

## The Third Challenge

or

## Go to Next Page

# Last Chance

Dear reader,

If you haven't already, this is the last chance to download our *All-Time Top 5 Bestselling* Guides for you absolutely free for you absolutely free as a part of this purchase.

Just enter where you want the books to be digitally delivered.

Enter Best Email Address Here

We hope you have enjoyed this book. Please take a moment to leave a review of this book at the end and share your experience.

Editor at
**WhizBooks**

Lightning Source UK Ltd.
Milton Keynes UK
UKHW021838111019
351423UK00011B/1216/P